The U.S. Supreme Court

by Mari Schuh

Consulting Editor: Gail Saunders-Smith, PhD

Consultant: Steven S. Smith, Kate M. Gregg Distinguished Professor
of Social Sciences and Professor of Political Science
Director, Weidenbaum Center on the Economy, Government, and Public Policy
Washington University, St. Louis, Missouri

CAPSTONE PRESS
a capstone imprint

Pebble Plus is published by Capstone Press,
1710 Roe Crest Drive, North Mankato, Minnesota 56003.
www.capstonepub.com

Books published by Capstone Press are manufactured with paper
containing at least 10 percent post-consumer waste.

Library of Congress Cataloging-in-Publication Data
Schuh, Mari C., 1975–
  The U.S. Supreme Court / by Mari Schuh.
     p. cm.—(Pebble plus. U.S. government)
  Includes bibliographical references and index.
  Summary: "Simple text and full-color photographs provide a brief introduction to the U.S. Supreme Court"—Provided
by publisher.
  ISBN 978-1-4296-7568-0 (library binding)
  1. United States. Supreme Court—Juvenile literature. 2. United States. Supreme Court. I. Title.
  KF8742.S288 2012
  347.73'26—dc23   2011021664

Editorial Credits
Erika L. Shores, editor; Ashlee Suker, designer; Kathy McColley, production specialist

Photo Credits
AP Images/Dana Verkouteren, 7, 17, 19, 21
newscom/Getty Images/AFP/Mandel Ngan, 11; Getty Images/AFP/Tim Sloan, cover, 13; Jeff Malet Photography, 9
Shutterstock/Gary Blakeley, 1, 5; Onur ERSIN, 15

Artistic Effects
Shutterstock: Christophe BOISSON

The author dedicates this book to Jadyn Friedrichs of Sioux City, Iowa.

Note to Parents and Teachers

The U.S. Government series supports national history standards related to understanding the
importance of and basic principles of American democracy. This book describes and illustrates
the U.S. Supreme Court. The images support early readers in understanding the text. The
repetition of words and phrases helps early readers learn new words. This book also introduces
early readers to subject-specific vocabulary words, which are defined in the Glossary section.
Early readers may need assistance to read some words and to use the Table of Contents,
Glossary, Read More, Internet Sites, and Index sections of the book.

Printed in the United States of America in North Mankato, Minnesota.
102011   006405CGS12

Table of Contents

The Highest Court

The Supreme Court in

Washington, D.C., decides

important court cases.

It is the most powerful court

in the United States.

The U.S. government has

three branches.

The judicial branch explains laws.

The Supreme Court is part

of the judicial branch.

Congress is the legislative branch. It makes laws. The executive branch makes sure people obey the laws.

Becoming a Justice

The president chooses justices

for the Supreme Court.

Then the Senate votes

on the president's choice.

Nine justices serve on the Supreme Court. Justices serve for life or until they retire.

The Court at Work

The Supreme Court decides

if laws follow the Constitution.

Some cases are about privacy,

religion, and freedom of speech.

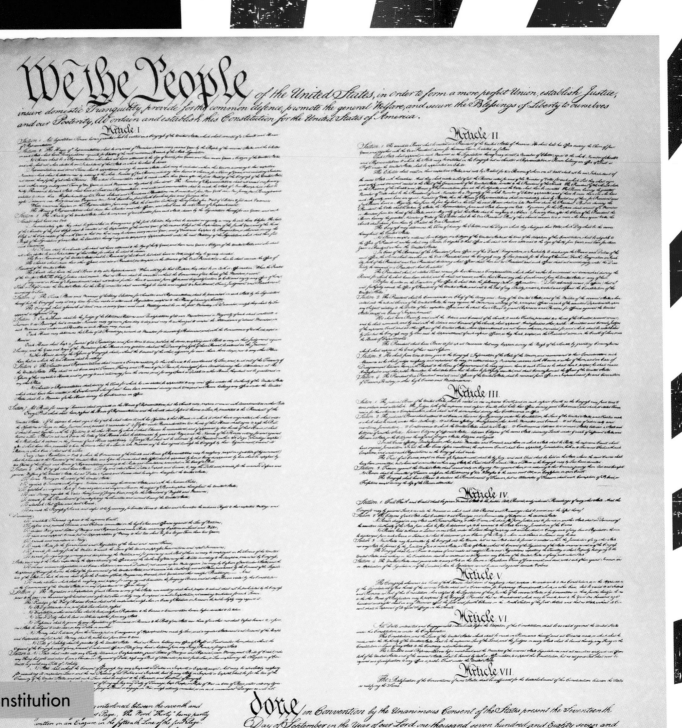

The U.S. Constitution

15

The Supreme Court rules

on about 75 cases each year.

The Supreme Court hears cases

that were first decided

by other courts.

Justices hear lawyers tell
their side of the case.
Justices meet about the case
and vote. Then justices write
opinions to explain their ruling.

The Supreme Court's ruling

in a case is final.

Sometimes the court's rulings

cause Congress to change laws

or make new laws.

Glossary

case—a legal problem settled in court

Congress—the part of the U.S. government that makes laws; Congress makes up the legislative branch of government; the Senate and the House of Representatives make up Congress

Constitution—a document that explains the system of laws and government in the United States

executive branch—the part of the U.S. government that makes sure people follow the laws; the president leads the executive branch

freedom of speech—the right to share ideas and beliefs without government control

justice—one of nine judges who decide cases brought before the U.S. Supreme Court

law—a rule made by the government that must be obeyed

legislative branch—the part of the U.S. government that makes laws

Read More

Fingeroth, Danny. *The U.S. Supreme Court.* Cartoon Nation. Mankato, Minn.: Capstone Press, 2009.

Harris, Nancy. *What's the Supreme Court?* First Guide to Government. Chicago: Heinemann Library, 2008.

Suen, Anastasia. *The U.S. Supreme Court.* American Symbols. Minneapolis: Picture Window Books, 2009.

Internet Sites

FactHound offers a safe, fun way to find Internet sites related to this book. All of the sites on FactHound have been researched by our staff.

Here's all you do:

Visit *www.facthound.com*

Type in this code: 9781429675680

Super-cool stuff! Check out projects, games and lots more at **www.capstonekids.com**

Index

Word Count: 175
Grade: 1
Early-Intervention Level: 20